Rookie Read-About® Science

Mirror, Mirror

By Allan Fowler

Consultants:
Robert L. Hillerich, Professor Emeritus,
Bowling Green State University, Bowling Green, Ohio
Consultant, Pinellas County Schools, Florida

Lynne Kepler, Educational Consultant

Fay Robinson, Child Development Specialist

CHILDRENS PRESS®
CHICAGO

Design by Beth Herman Design Associates

Library of Congress Cataloging-in-Publication Data

Fowler, Allan.
    Mirror, mirror / by Allan Fowler.
        p. cm. – (Rookie read-about science)
        ISBN 0-516-06023-6
        1. Reflection (Optics)–Juvenile literature. 2. Mirrors–Juvenile literature.
    [1. Reflection (Optics) 2. Mirrors.] I. Title. II. Series: Fowler, Allan.
    Rookie read-about science.
    QC425.2.F68   1994
    535'323–dc20   93-38591
                                                            CIP
                                                             AC

A long time ago, before there were any glass mirrors . . . how did people know what they looked like?

In the still water of a
pond or brook,

4

a person would see a face
looking back . . . and realize
it was his or her own face
shining off the water.

When light hits a surface, it bounces back. This is called a reflection.

Smooth, shiny surfaces, like water, produce the best reflections.

Water was the first mirror.

Later, people used polished metal to reflect their faces.

Finally, they discovered
a way to get an even
clearer reflection.

They covered one side
of a piece of clear glass
with a silvery coating.

11

We'd have a hard time getting along without mirrors. Actors need mirrors when they put on makeup.

So does a clown.

A man may need the
bathroom mirror
when he shaves.

You may use a mirror
when you try on new
clothes or comb your hair.

A big mirror on the
wall makes a room
seem larger.

It looks as if the room
is twice as big.

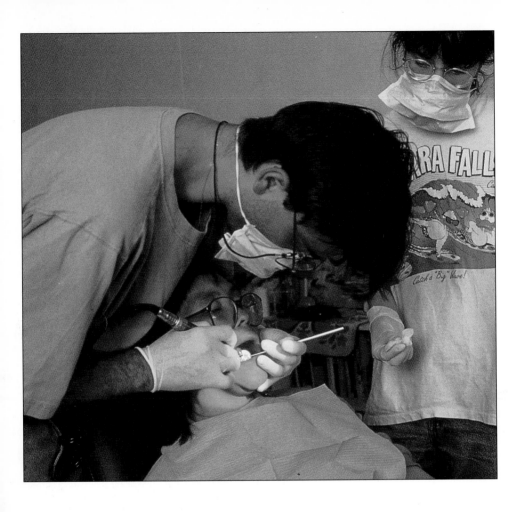

A dentist uses a little mirror
to see the back of your teeth.

You can use mirrors to
see around corners.

A rearview mirror lets a
driver see what is behind
the car.

A periscope is a long tube
with a mirror at each end.
It allows the crew of a
submarine to see what's
on the surface of the water.

When you see
things reflected,
they look backward.

Write your name on a piece of paper. Hold it up to a mirror. What do you see?

Mirrors reflect things.
But mirrors can fool you too.

If a mirror is curved instead
of flat, it does funny things
to your reflection.

A fun-house mirror might
make you look like this . . .

or
like
this.

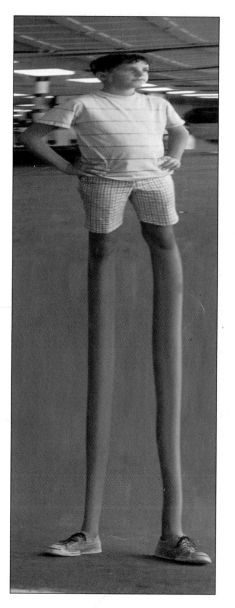

If you stand in front of more than one mirror, you see more than one reflection of yourself.

But don't worry. There's only one of you.

Do you like what you see?

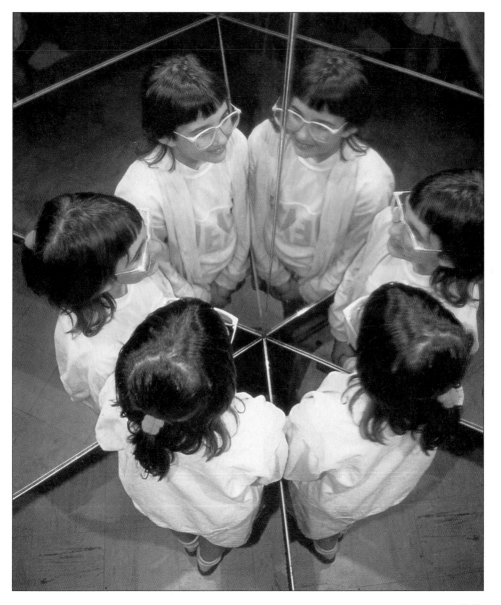

Words You Know

reflection

water

mirror

rearview mirror

submarine periscope

toy periscope

curved mirror

Index

About the Author

Allan Fowler is a free-lance writer with a background in advertising. Born in New York, he lives in Chicago now and enjoys traveling.

Photo Credits

The Bettmann Archive – 4, 11
Carolina Mirror Company – 17
PhotoEdit – ©Jeff Greenberg, cover; ©Deborah Davis, 8; ©David Young-Wolff, 23; ©Tony Freeman, 14, 15, 21, 25, 26, 29, 31 (center right and bottom)
Photri – 31 (center left); ©Curtis Martin, 19; ©Lani Novak Howe, 22, 24
©Carl Purcell – 27
SuperStock International, Inc. – ©L. Willinger, 13, 30 (bottom right); ©Neil Slavin, 20, 31 (top)
Valan – ©J.A. Wilkinson, 5, 30 (top); ©Dennis W. Schmidt, 7; ©John Eastcott/Yva Momatiuk, 12, 18; ©Jeff Foott, 30 (bottom left)
COVER: Child looks in mirror.